THEY DID ALL THE DIRTY WORK IN ANCIENT GREECE
Slaves and Soldiers

Ancient History Illustrated
Children's Ancient History

Speedy Publishing LLC

40 E. Main St. #1156

Newark, DE 19711

www.speedypublishing.com

Copyright 2017

Slavery was common during the era of Ancient Greece. Many families had at least one slave and they were a key part of the Ancient Greece economy and culture.

The city-states of Ancient Greece would often fight against each other and groups would often unite in fighting in large wars with other groups of city-states.

Ancient Greek Warrior

Ancient Greek Warrior

In this book, we will be learning about how the slaves and the soldiers became a part of the history of Ancient Greece.

DID THE GREEKS HAVE A LOT OF SLAVES?

Historians are not exactly sure as to the number of slaves that the Greeks owned, but it is estimated that somewhere between 30 to 40 percent of the Greek population consisted of slaves. Even the poor families would own at least one slave and the wealthy families might own hundreds. The slave owner would be responsible for any crime that their slave may have committed. Many times, the wealthy Greeks would purchase slaves as an investment and turn around and rent them to others.

Antic Slave Market

WHERE DID THE
SLAVES COME FROM?

Many of them were foreigners that were captured during war or purchased by slave trade. Often, they would be captured by bandits or pirates and then sold at a slave market.

WHAT TYPE OF WORK DID THEY PERFORM?

The slaves would perform a variety of tasks depending on who owned them and what skills they could do. Some would perform hard labor on farms or in mines. Others would do household chores or work as artisans in the city. Mining was the worst job for the slaves. It was hard work and dangerous and the slaves that worked in the mines did not have a long life span.

Ruins of Paliapoli

Delphi with Ruins of the Temple in Greece

DID THEY HAVE RIGHTS?

In Ancient Greece, there were various types of slaves and varying rules depending on what city they lived in. In general, however, they had very few rights. They would have to work long hours doing whatever their owner demanded they do. They could not own any property and slaves had less rights than citizens.

WERE THEY EVER SET FREE?

Occasionally, the slaves would be set free by their owners, known as manumission. Owners could also allow them to save money and purchase their freedom. Once they were freed, they still were not considered to be full citizens and would often still be obliged to their former owners.

Sardeis Temple of Artemis

Lindos Village

HOW DID THEY KNOW THE DIFFERENCE BETWEEN A SLAVE AND A FREE PERSON?

Sometimes it was difficult to tell a slave from a free person. Often, slave women would have short hair, which marked them as a slave since free women in Ancient Greece would have long hair. The slaves sometimes were marked with tattoos or scars so they would be recognizable as a slave.

SLAVES OF THE SPARTANS

Helots were a group of people the Spartans ruled over, and were treated as slaves. They would farm the land and perform other manual type labors for the Spartans. Actually, there were many more Helots than there were Spartans.

Spartan Warrior

Spartan Warrior

To maintain control, the Spartans had a secret police force to keep track of the Helots and they would kill anyone that might rebel. Every year the Spartans would declare war on the Helots so they were able to kill them and it would not be considered as murder.

WHO WERE THE SOLDIERS?

All men that lived in a Greek city-state were required to fight in the army. In many cases, they were not full-time soldiers, but men that owned businesses or land and they were fighting in defense of their property.

Ancient Greece

Ancient Greek Warrior

WHAT ARMOR AND WEAPONS DID THEY USE?

Each warrior would have to provide their own weapons and armor. The wealthier soldiers would typically have better weapons and armor. Included with a full set of armors would be a helmet, a shield, a bronze breastplate, and greaves that were used to protect the shins. Most of them would carry a long spear known as a doru and a short spear known as a xiphos.

A complete set of weapons and arms would be quite heavy and weight more than 60 pounds. The shield by itself could weigh as much as 30 pounds and was considered to be the most significant part of the soldier's armor. It would be considered as a disgrace for a soldier to lose their shield during battle. Legend tells us that the Spartan mothers would tell their sons to return home "with their shield or on it" which meant they had to be wearing their shield or, if they were dead, they would often be carried on their shield.

Occasionally, these soldiers would decorate their shields and a common symbol placed on the shields of the Athens' soldiers was a small owl that represented Athena, a goddess.

Other weapons they used were archers and javelin throwers. The "sarissa", introduced by Philip II of Macedon, was a longer spear, about 20 feet long, and weighed about 14 pounds.

Philip II of Macedon

Hoplite Fight from Athens Museum

HOPLITES

Hoplites were the main Greek soldier that was the foot soldier. They would carry long spears and large shields. The term "hoplite" came from their shields which they referred to as "hoplon".

PHALANX

The battle formation the hoplites fought in during battle was known as the "phalanx". When the soldiers were in the phalanx, they would stand side by side while overlapping their shields, forming a wall for protection. They would then march forward while using their spears in attacking their opponents. Generally, there would be many rows of soldiers. The soldiers that were located towards the rear would brace the soldiers toward the front and also would keep moving forward.

Greek Phalanx

As two phalanxes would come together during battle, their goal was to break apart the enemy's phalanx. The battles would often become somewhat of a pushing match and the first phalanx to break would typically lose the battle.

Greek Phalanx

THE SPARTANS

The Spartans were the fiercest and most famous warriors of Ancient Greece. They were known as a warrior society and each man trained as a soldier from when he was just a young boy. Each one would go through a difficult boot camp training. The Spartan men were required to train to be soldiers and to fight until they reached the age of 60.

Spartan Warrior

Old Greek Trireme

FIGHTING AT SEA

The Greeks were known to be experts at building ships since they lived along the Aegean Sea coast. The trireme was one of the key ships used during battle. It had three oar banks along each side which allowed up to 170 rowers to man and power the ship, which made this ship very fast during battle.

The bronze prow was the main weapon aboard a Greek ship and was located towards the front of the ship. It was made to be used similar to a battering ram. Sailors would ram it into the side of the enemy's ship, which would cause it to sink.

Ancient Greek Warship

Statue of Alexander the Great

ANCIENT GREECE

Ancient Greece was known to be the civilization that controlled most of the Mediterranean thousands of years ago and ruled most of Western Asia and Europe under Alexander the Great. The Greeks came prior to the Romans and most of the Roman culture had been shaped by the Greeks.

Everything from literature, art, government, science, philosophy, and even sports was impacted by the Ancient Greeks as well as the foundation of most of today's Western culture.

Ancient Greek Temple Frieze

The Erechtheion Temple in Athens

TIME PERIODS

Ancient Greece history is often divided up into three eras, the Archaic Period, the Classical Period, and the Hellenistic Period.

The Archaic Period began in 800 BC with Greek civilization and ran through 508 BC, which was the beginning of Democracy. The start of the Olympics, as well as Homer's writing, Odyssey and the Illiad, took place during this time period.

Parthenon

Plato and Socrates

The Classical Period is the time that we mostly think about when we think about Ancient Greece. Great philosophers such as Plato and Socrates arose and Athens was governed by a democracy. The wars between Athens and Sparta occurred during this era. It ended in 323 BC with the rise and death of Alexander the Great.

The Hellenistic Period started with the death of Alexander the Great and lasted until Rome conquered Greece in 146 BC. The word Hellenistic arises from the Greek word "hellens", which is how the Greeks referred to themselves.

Sardeis Temple of Artemis

Ancient Greek Ruins at Sparta

SPARTA AND ATHENS

Sparta and Athens were the two major city-states which ruled most of Ancient Greece. Often, they would be adversaries and fought against each other in the Peloponnesian Wars. They united at different times in order to protect the Greek lands from any attackers. The cultures of these cities were quite different. While Athens was focused more on learning and the arts, Sparta was mostly focused on war.

There is so much more to learn about Ancient Greece, the slaves, the soldiers and the wars. It is all quite interesting. For additional information, you can go to your local library, research the internet, and ask questions of your teachers, family and friends.

Visit
BABY PROFESSOR
EDUCATION KIDS
www.BabyProfessorBooks.com
to download Free Baby Professor eBooks
and view our catalog of new and exciting
Children's Books